Body Language

The Ultimate Guide to Read, Connect, Influence, Attract, and Analyze Anyone Instantly with Your Non-Verbal Communication

Table of Contents

Introduction

Think of all our best actors and actresses. What is it exactly that makes them "best"? They are masters of both voice and body language! They are masters of vocal communication and communicating via their entire body. With every new character they portray, their verbal and nonverbal communication via their body changes – often dramatically.

There are other actors about whom we say, "There he goes, playing himself again." My guess is that we really mean his use of his voice and his body is static, immobile, and inflexible. He gives us the same character in every film he does. Because he gives us the only voice he knows and uses the only body language he knows – his own.

Remember all those police procedural TV shows and films that you have seen. All those detective novels that you have read. The best detectives portrayed in them are masters at reading voice inflections, facial tics, and overall body language of the suspect. In real life, whole careers are made on an individual's ability to not only read the voice and the body language of the bad guy – but to be right about their interpretations. Interviewers, interrogators, and profilers have mastered the interpretation of nonverbal communication of others. This helps them catch out the liars or detect when someone is holding back information or perhaps protecting another person.

And what about those public speakers who have you on the edge of your chair, your mouth hanging open or your eyes wide? Are you spellbound only from the *words* they are saying? Absolutely not! Their nonverbal communication is part of that whole package they are giving you. How they walk the stage. What they do with their hands and arms. How they bend or stretch their body or reach out. Their facial expressions as they speak. It's all a package deal to become what their public calls "a charismatic speaker."

There is really no way around it: The most successful, influential individuals are masters not only of the spoken word but of body language. They use

nonverbal skills of their own – but also a

bang-on interpretation of yours – to get

things done by persuading you to seek them out, hear them out, do things for or with them and buy their gizmos. They are influential because they give you what you need in the way your own body language says you need it. They get along with most everyone since they read you correctly and adapt to you (rather than demanding the reverse).

Throughout this book, you will find sections entitled Do It. I will be giving you the opportunity to be that actor or that profiler or that charismatic spellbinder who is calling on his ability to read and understand as well as use body language.

Chapter 1: A Gesture Speaks Volumes

How People Communicate

A picture is worth 1,000 words. We have all heard that expression and it is true. Part of how humans paint pictures is with their bodies. We call it *body language*. In this age of cinema and social media videos, we are exposed from morning to night to examples of body language.

How do we register body language in others? I say "register", because it is so very often an unconscious recognition. Unconsciously, we notice some sort of body language, which leads us to (sub)consciously react to it.

That humans register body language unconsciously is very interesting to realize: Could you learn all about body language and get people to act and react the way you *want* them to? You most certainly could. Like the professionals in the Introduction (whose job it is to get you to react to their nonverbal communication or to correctly interpret that of others), you can learn to use your own body language to influence others.

But first, we go back to the old rule that says, "Know thyself." Your first job is to study your own body language. Some of your current nonverbal communication is already highly effective in helping you get what you want. Other aspects of your body language are sabotaging you in your effort to get what you want – whether you realize it or not.

To start your study, let's look at the major components of body language. All of my examples in this chapter will be within the North American culture. As we will see in the next chapter, body language is not universal but is culture-derived.

Body Space

Nonverbal communication starts with the amount of empty space you require around your body as well as the amount of space you give other people. It is all about comfort and respect.

If we are with strangers or people we simply don't know very well, we like to preserve an arm's length distance. And this is actually where the expression,

"He kept me at arm's length" comes

from! It means, "He treated me like a stranger."

This rule presents real difficulties in some of our urban situations, such as taking a crowded elevator or public transportation. There is not enough room to maintain arm's length space around our body. All you need to do is observe people in this situation to see how we deal with this invasion of our space. In an elevator, we make sure to nod to the other people or to quietly speak our standard greeting of "good morning" or "how are you?" Those few words and that quiet nod are *cultural signals* to others that we are protecting the space around us as best we can. Notice how our tradition of shaking hands in more formal situations also keeps us at a (double) arm's-length from each other!

Even if we are quite friendly or even intimate with individuals, reducing our body space must be mutual. Touching must be mutual. And it's easy if you are attentive to the other person's body language to know if they agree or not!

Facial Communication

Facial communication is fun to observe, analyze and imitate! Did you realize that you can smile in several different ways? Think about it for a moment. Which parts of your face can you smile with?

1. She had a twinkle in her <u>eye</u>.

2. Not smiling at all, he laughed with his <u>eyes</u> and his <u>body</u> jiggled with glee right along with it.

3. He had a smile that <u>didn't go</u> to his eyes.

4. Her <u>whole face</u> lit up when she smiled.

In the first two examples, the smile happens in the eyes alone. However, the nonverbal message is quite different. In #1, the rest of her face and body is not involved in the smile, but you might suspect that she has a delightful secret behind those eyes. In #2, the fellow is trying to keep from laughing out loud by *not* smiling – but his body is a dead giveaway that he's ready to burst with laughter. #3 is an insincere smile, and you may find you do not trust what this person says or does. Further reading of his body may show a sadness, and his eyes show they simply have no will or energy to go along with his attempt at a smile. In #4, the person's entire face participated in the smile which is genuine; the human face only "lights up" when the smile is genuine and even expresses joy or delight along with it.

Here is a hint for you travelers: A *genuine, happy* smile is universal!

Body Posture and Position

Here is a good point that needs attention. As in example #3, your whole body must be *congruent* with the message you are trying to communicate. In that example, an observer immediately understands the fellow is not happy – he is only making an

attempt to smile. That might be for any number of reasons. But when the smile he puts on his mouth is contradicted by everything else he does with his *body*, you read the rest of his body to understand his real message. With this type of smile, you have to add in the rest of what you observe his body doing. Is he 1) reluctant, 2) sad, 3) angry? To find out, look at the rest of his body language:

1. Reluctant: His eyes are frowning. He's making a push-away gesture with both hands and arms.

2. Sad: His whole body is slack. The muscles around his eyes are loose,

his whole body looks like it would collapse like a ragdoll.

3. Angry: His eyes are blazing, his face is tense, and maybe his jaw is clenched. All his muscles are ready for battle, even to the point of making fists.

These contradictions are also a big part of nonverbal communication. You may consciously decide to display contradictory body language because it serves your purpose and message. In other circumstances, it may serve your purpose and message to have a unified body language. The real question is what you wish to communicate. What is your message? What are you trying to achieve?

Movement of Extremities

There is something interesting about body language, the mind, and our extremities. Even individuals aware of their body language and in pretty good control of it, tend to ignore what's happening with their arms and legs! There is a theory that the further the body part is away from the mind (head), the less attention the individual pays to what's happening. So it behooves you to identify the body language of your own arms and legs and to closely observe how other people use their arms and legs to support or contradict their messages.

Look at any speaker trying to get his audience to follow him, to see him as an authority figure or accept him as their leader. At a lectern or on the podium, his feet are planted about 2 feet apart in a sort of military "at rest" stance and he rarely moves. His arms do not move very much either but are placed wide from his body so that he seems to take up more space than he needs. His hands do not flail around, but his palms often face the audience with fingers spread. This has an effect of pulling the audience in toward him – making him and the audience a unit. It is the position of power used by many true leaders when they speak.

On the other hand, a speaker unskilled in body language may fold his arms across his rib cage, and thus separate or protect himself from his listeners. He's pushing them out and away from him. This might communicate that the audience is not good enough for him, or that he's uncomfortable with them, or that he does not need them. This same speaker may nervously pace a stage or the front of the room. This communicates a lack of preparation to talk about the subject at hand. Such a speaker may also not be in control of his facial expressions and other tics. In such a case, he may frown to contradict the words he's saying. He may make a smile that does not reach his eyes, which may depict that the unfortunate thing he is saying is true – or that he is simply lying to the crowd.

The power speaker may be totally unconscious that he is using power positions for his arms and legs. But this body language can be learned. The weaker speaker may have no knowledge of body language at all – or his extreme nervousness might cancel all his knowledge out.

Of course, none of these examples is carved in stone. You need to put the whole package together.

Look for these individual postures or positioning of the body:

Legs

•When sitting with another individual, crossing the outer leg toward the other person is a sign that you're comfortable and welcoming to the individual. Doing the reverse by crossing the leg nearest to that person away from him expresses separation or some kind of disconnect or disinterest.

•Tapping your foot (in non-musical circumstances!) is a sign of nervousness or impatience.

•Jiggling the feet is a subconscious desire to run away from whatever is happening – to avoid the topic being discussed or the people nearby.

•Standing with one leg/foot forward depends on circumstances. If the foot is pointed toward an exit, the person wants to get away. It is also a posture of showing status, as if to say, look at my fine shoes and clothing. However, if the hand is on the hip at the same time, it might show a bit of arrogance or impatience.

In each of these examples, remember to look at the rest of the body! Body language is a package deal.

Your Arms

People really have difficulties controlling the body language of their arms and hands. That can be a real drawback because:

- When you cross your arms across your chest, that can show and unwillingness – to listen, to participate, to believe the speaker, to do what is asked.

- In our culture, when you flail your hands around as you speak, it is a sign of nervousness or a wish to overdramatize. It can also communicate that you feel out of control … or simply seek attention.

- When a teenager sits on his hands – in combination with keeping a sulky head bowed – you are never connecting with him. Maybe he's bored or perhaps resisting whatever is happening during this situation. He might also be afraid of reprisals or disciplinary action and is trying to make himself a small as possible.

- Tapping your fingers on your lap or a tabletop or worse yet, using the tabletop as a drum for your whole palm can mean a lot of things according to the context. What it does not mean is that the person is patiently paying attention ! The person is impatient, nervous, disinterested.

Nervous Tics

Remember the Harry Potter film villain Barty Crouch Junior? He was the one with the memorable tic of darting his tongue out of the side of his mouth from nervousness. Any time he sensed that the jig was up for him, he would dart his tongue. As you watch films and videos, you have plenty of opportunities to watch for nervous tics and what triggers them in the individual.

Maybe your left eye twitches when you get tired. Anyone who knows you realizes you're tired when your eyes start twitching. Your wife or your boyfriend might send you off to bed for a nap when they notice it. Your boss? Not so much.

Tapping your fingers might be something you do when you disagree with whatever someone is saying. Your best friends and family understand this – and might even wickedly push that button of yours more often than usual to rile you up.

Jiggling your feet might be unconscious behavior on your part. Those who know you best realize the meaning – you want to leave the place that you're in because you're bored out of your mind. Again, too bad. Your boss doesn't recognize the meaning of this tic of yours!

Nervous tics are nothing more than body language outside your control at this time. Pull them back into your control, through awareness and practice.

If you are to know yourself and your own body language, you will have to get the assistance of some good friends to point out your nervous tics to you. If you are together with someone quite frequently, he can use a code word when you have your nervous tic behavior. When you hear that word, you are supposed to stop doing it. It's just a matter of attention and practice.

As you observe another person's nervous tic, you naturally do not call it to his attention! Just watch, and from the context of the situation, try to make an intelligent guess about what that tic really means.

Control It

You can bring your own body language, including your nervous tics, into your personal control by committing to quiet observation of yourself and others, and to practice in front of the mirror.

Who should learn to identify his own body language? Who should learn how others in his culture react and act to his own body language?

If you have confusion in social situations, it may be body language! If you just don't understand why people walk away from you when you start to speak, examine your body language –

and theirs. If you are terrified to speak

in front of people of authority (your boss, elders in your family, government people), examine your own body language. If you generally feel that people don't pay attention to you, it's body language.

But it is a two-way street. You can do everything you want to master interpreting other people's body language. But if you don't know what your own body language is communicating, you are sabotaging yourself. Know thyself! Observe others.

Bringing your body language under your control – and correctly interpreting other people's nonverbal communication – has great benefits:

- more self-confidence
- ability to influence others
- ability to respond more appropriately and successfully

Do It!

1. Check out what an "arm's length" represents for you and others in different situations in public and with strangers.

2. Try all four types of smile. Try first without a mirror, then see what it looks like in one.

3. If you are not a person who smiles naturally, start practicing. A genuine smile from a happy body makes life easier, smooths your way, opens doors, makes others comfortable. Practice, practice, practice!

4. Ask those closest to you if you have any nervous tics. Yes, you might already know what they are. Use the "code word" system with a loved one to tackle them.

Chapter 2: Body Language and Culture – Traveler Beware!

Photographs, paintings and other types of visuals are so effective at communicating a message across cultures. But what exactly is the message communicated? Is the same message received in Borneo as in Brazil as in Berlin from the same picture? That is the question…

Within your culture, each one of your gestures and facial expressions, each one of your body's movements communicates a message which is correctly interpreted by those who see it.

Outside of your culture, this is not always so. One size definitely does not fit all when it comes to body language. Nonverbal communication is far from being universal. In other words, be *aware* that the same gesture or facial expression means different things in different cultures. It may be totally safe to use some gestures in your culture, but the very same ones will get you in hot water or worse in other parts of the world!

How much empty space we need around our bodies to feel respected and secure differs from culture to culture, as does the amount of physical touching that strangers will find appropriate. The nonverbal messages communicated through clothing choices are also quite different around the globe. Not all facial expressions communicate the same idea or feelings either.

Gestures

In Italy, there is a lot of *hand and arm touching* or patting on the back during ordinary conversation – when "ordinary" may include loud voices and arm waving. This is all considered quite friendly. In Japan, however, this *touching and loudness* would be considered not only quite rude and disrespectful – it would be outright disconcerting to be treated this way.

Men in the Middle East may be seen walking, talking together and *holding hands* in a corridor or even on the street. No, they are not romantic partners! In these cultures, it is a sign of respect. On the other hand, in Western Europe or North America, two adult gentlemen *holding hands* in public signifies their intimate relationship to each other, with the assumption that they are gay. Yet two French girls walking down the street holding hands has no other connotation but friendship.

How you gesture for someone to *come toward* you varies from country to country. In France, you would extend your arm, palm down toward the floor and make a scooping motion with your hand. In the United States, you would extend your arm palm upward toward the ceiling and make a vigorous upward scooping motion. In the US, you might also just crook your index finger from a palm up and fingers folded position. You might even whistle. This is considered an outright insult in other countries!

Body language also includes things you *carry*. As an example, in Brazil, whenever you are carrying anything (spare clothing, books, food items), it is expected to be *wrapped* in a paper or stored in a carry bag. In France, however, you'll see the young and old leave the bakery with a naked baguette in their hands. *No wrapping*! They'll even go so far as to carry it on the subway trains with them or lay it on the seat of the car if they're driving. This practice is disconcerting to sanitation-conscious Japanese and American observers!

Clothing

Your choice of *clothing styles and its condition* is a strong nonverbal message to others. We are mostly aware that in some cultures females of any age are expected to be fully covered with clothing from head to toe – and sometimes that includes the face. But that is not universal either since it is reasonably acceptable for girls through the high school age to go to school in spaghetti strap tank tops and short shorts in Hawaii.

Think about this – the Japanese bow frequently as a salutation to each other. What do they see first when they do this? Your *shoes*! Are they polished to a high sheen and in good condition? Better be, if you are trying to make a good impression because down at the heel and dusty shoes communicate an entirely different nonverbal message from well-maintained shoes.

In the traditional Middle East, the father may refuse (or pretend not) to recognize his daughter in public when she is *bare-headed*; it is a sign of her respect for cultural and religious tradition to *cover her head*, but also a sign of respect to her elders. This is not an issue in Northern Europe or the US.

And what clothing signals that a female is "*available*" in your culture?

Remember that it changes from country to country! American casual wear for females may just signal your sexual availability to someone from another culture. The mildest reaction you may get in that country is lots of giggles, pointing and laughter; the most dangerous one you get may be a man grabbing you and beating you with his hands (or worse) – because your clothing signaled you should not be out in public. Beware!

Face

The British stiff upper lip really is formed on the face. Its message is, "I am in control of my feelings, no matter how bad it gets." Other British who see that may say, "That fellow must be really emotional, but at least he is not collapsing from his feelings *in public*." However, for other cultures that same stiff upper lip is an expression of coldness and a total lack of emotions – and is thus very off-putting.

While these few examples all represent notable differences from one culture to another, some body language is shared amongst a huge number of societies. For instance, when the face shows happiness or sadness, fear or anger, or repulsion or surprise – numerous

peoples around the world understand what is written on that face. And did you know that people born blind also express these emotions with exactly the same facial expressions as their sighted fellowman? That is truly universal!

Sure, there are some differences. North Americans will express the positive as well as the negative emotions both privately and in public. The Japanese, however, tend to express the negative feelings on their face only in private.

The facial expressions are the same nonetheless.

Rest assured that when you smile with your mouth, your cheeks and your eyes (and you have no other body language that contradicts it) – almost everyone around the world will understand that you are expressing happiness and approval, and maybe great joy! Also, be aware that if your smile is not sincere, most people will *also* be able to read *that*.

Learn

Before you travel outside your own culture, get knowledgeable. There is plenty of information on the Internet giving you nonverbal communication cues country by country. Look for cues about covering your head and acceptable types of clothing, how loud voices are received, how to gesture appropriately when you need something or someone, and so on. Other types of nonverbal communication include knowing how and how much to pay or tip for goods or services. Practice all of this before leaving home, so that you don't fumble with it too much. But most especially? Practice your most sincere eyes+cheeks+mouth smiles. This said, also check when smiling may *not* be appropriate at all in the country you are visiting!

Do It!

Find a <u>foreign</u> film on YouTube or television. Watch 15 or 20 minutes of it at a time, *with the volume muted.* Jot down what you notice about body language, using the following guidelines:

1. Look at their hand and arm gestures. Which feelings and emotions do those seem to express? If you translated those gestures into words, what would they be?

2. Facial expressions, as you already know, also express feelings. Think anger, excitement, happiness,

sadness, fear and so on. What do those seem to communicate (what would the spoken message be)?

3. Notice how the actors handle props, carry things or hold them. What attitude or message can they be expressing? For example, repulsion at having to carry such a thing, awkwardness at holding a cumbersome item, etc.

4. Whether a modern film or historic one, look at the choice of clothing amongst the characters. What is clothing used to portray? Wealth and affluence, poverty, a working man with a specific profession? Usually, one glance gives you this kind of information.

Chapter 3: Reading North American Body Language

Disclaimer: Reading body language within your own culture is *not an exact* <u>science</u>. Anyone who says it is, is trying to make himself look more expert than he is. In fact, if you teamed with friends or family to complete the Do It! exercises of chapter 2 – you probably noticed that you interpreted that foreign body language differently from each other. Does that tell you anything about the risks of traveling abroad and jumping to conclusions? It should!

This certainly doesn't mean that you cannot develop some skill in reading the people at home that you are around the most often. It's always best to start with your own body language because then you are in tune with what to look for in other people. Then start practicing with your family members. Be analytical. Don't assume that because you know them so well... that you know them so well! A study of a sister's or an uncle's body language may reveal aspects of these individuals you never considered before.

Eye Contact

We haven't discussed eye contact at all yet. In our culture, nonverbal experts believe that the eyes speak volumes – if only we knew how to read them.

You don't need to understand about pupil dilation and some of the more theoretical aspects in order to benefit from observing how people use their eyes.

What does it mean when someone avoids eye contact with you? They're hiding some feeling or are ashamed of some action that you are speaking of. They may feel insecure and are preparing for rejection, by cringing their eyes away from you. It might also simply mean that you are distracting them while they are trying to do something else or watch for someone else coming toward them.

An individual pierces you with his continuous eye contact, constantly glaring directly into your eyes. What is this about? Some young Romeo may believe that this is romantic, or another eager beaver might believe this is the best way to show that he is attentively listening to you. Or this might be an angry individual trying to be threatening. In our culture, this eye language is actually quite intimidating! If this is one of your habits, stop it.

If a person of authority is sitting at a desk writing or keyboarding, without making eye contact with you, he is probably doing one of two things. You are interrupting him; he has made a decision to focus on his work rather than on you, and his lack of eye contact confirms that. Alternatively, he's trying to show you who's boss – you are not important enough for him to turn away from his other vital work!

Men have a hard time with this one: Women crying. Fellows are always in a panic, asking themselves what they did to make her cry, wondering what's wrong or what terrible catastrophe has occurred. She's happy?! Maybe. It's all about context. Maybe she really is sad, aggrieved about something that's happened. And then again, as guys fear, it might be hormones. Good luck, fellows!

Blinking, winking. These are also commonly misunderstood eye language. Blinking can mean that the person is trying to figure something out before speaking, and is in suspension – sort of like a deer in the headlights. For some, blinking is flirtatious. So is winking when done between sexes on a date or other intimate setting, but in our culture, we need to be careful of context. One big eye wink between friends means, "I told you so" or "We're in agreement on that."

The meanings and messages that the eyes convey are numerous, and to understand, we need full context. What is the rest of the body doing, in other words? Experts have spent whole careers studying just this.

Head Positions and Movements

Shaking your head from left to right means "no" in North America. But that's not all it means! It might be an expression of amazement that the individual wasn't expecting to feel. It might mean, "I don't know what to do about this". A slower left-to-right headshaking, in the right context, might mean, "You haven't convinced me yet, I'm not a believer yet, so keep talking."

Nodding your head up and down means "yes" in our culture. But that's not all! It might mean, "Congratulations!" or "Brilliant idea!" in support of something just said. One brief nod might simply be a silent greeting to someone has entered the room or discrete acknowledgment that you have seen them. A slow up-and-down nod, again in the right context, might express understanding of some complex idea the other person is talking about, or just confirmation that you are listening intently.

Some people tilt their head when talking with one or more people. That might mean they like *you*, or only that they like the *conversation* they are having with you. This is interesting: Try changing topics; if the person is still looking at you with a tilted head, it's you they like, regardless of what you talk about!

There are many circumstances in which we lift our chin up or tuck it down into our neck. A sudden lift of the chin up, then down, might mean, "Aha! I finally understand your point." Lifting the chin and holding it up can mean anything from a reaction of arrogance pride, or superiority. But maybe you're just trying to clear your throat before speaking. It could be your best attempt to regain emotional control. In fact, many teachers of young children and counselors know this trick: If you feel like you're going to cry, lift your eyes and chin to the ceiling for a few moments. It is a trick to help control emotional overwhelm.

If the chin is tucked down into the neck, it is about seeking protection from outside threats or judgments – tucking

in is symbolic of protecting the throat from a physical punch. We also tuck our chin down and backwards with a grimace on our face to express strong revulsion or disgust.

Position and Posture of Body

Legs express territorialism. If a man is sitting in the *middle* of a long bench with his knees and feet far apart, he has claimed the whole bench for himself. Even if he spreads his arms along the back of the bench, he's on the lookout for people daring to encroach on his territory. Sure, he may be relaxed. But he wants to do it *alone*! On the other hand, anyone sitting on a *far edge* of the bench, no matter what their body position, is saying to others that seating on the rest of the bench is available. How often does someone in your household sprawl on the sofa after sitting right in the middle? What is your best guess – are they willing to share the sofa or not?

Upper body positions can express feelings or behavioral attitudes. At conference or dinner tables, many of us find ourselves propping our bodies up with one elbow on the table and our chin in that palm. Although it might just be a poor posture habit, how you *feel* at the time may also be communicated. If your upper body is slumped forward from the shoulders, and your head or eyes turned downward to the table – chances are you really don't want anyone to talk to you because you're not feeling up to it, or you're bored. Contrarily, if your upper body is held vertically with your shoulders back, your head is facing forward or upward from your palm, and you are gazing out into the room – chances are you're open for conversation, participation or just active listening. Think about how your family sits around your dinner table. Which people have one of these postures? Try to determine the meaning of that posture. Is it a bad habit? Try to see which feeling is expressed, whether the person is available for conversation or not, or is just plain fatigued.

The meaning of some body language may depend on more than one area of your body. What does your spouse or your parent mean when they stand, feet apart with their hands on their hips? I think you will agree it depends largely on their facial expression! Are they scowling at you in anger? That usually means someone's in for some scolding. That's a very different facial expression from when they look at you with a silly grin and shake their head at the same time their hands are on their hips. That might mean that they've fallen for one of your old jokes or tricks again, or you've turned a bad situation around with some kind of humor so that you don't get scolded.

We have said that words or verbal communication can be contradicted by body language or nonverbal communication. That boss of yours is focused on his computer screen and bent over the keyboard, as he speaks the words, "I'm listening to you, what is it?" It is his body language that tells you he's not really listening. The meaning when someone says the words, "I like that idea" while he is scowling and shaking his head may be confusing to interpret. You need the whole context. Is he scowling as if to say "about time!" Is he shaking his head in amazed wonderment that you actually came up with a fabulous idea? This is another case when you need the whole context. Otherwise, that individual's meaning is up for grabs.

Involuntary Tics

A huge number of people have what are known as involuntary tics – some body language that is (apparently) outside their awareness or control. These tics have almost become part of their personality if you think about it. Someone says "eye fluttering", and you think of your friend Marianne. Someone says "shoulder rolls", and you think of your buddy George. Although those tics may exist for purely physiological reasons, what is their message? When does Marianne get triggered to do the eye fluttering or George to roll his shoulders?

There is no need to call your friends' attention to these tics (or that you are aware of them), but it does help you to notice them in people and to try to identify their triggers. Chalk it up to you, learning more and more about body language!

Do It!

1. For the language of your eyes to serve you, spend two or three minutes every time you are in a meeting or a group to notice what your own eyes are doing. Are they

downcast or scanning the group?
Are they staring down a hated co-
worker when he says something
stupid? When you are speaking,
where are your eyes? Where are
they when you are listening? Be
observant and notice the result
that each of these signals creates
for you.

2. As you notice everything in #1,
also make a note of your comfort
level. How comfortable are you
when your eyes are downcast as
versus scanning the group? What
is your degree of comfort in
making eye contact as you speak to
a specific person? Perhaps you
notice that you avoid making eye
contact entirely. When you are
speaking to a group, do you make
eye contact with each of the

individuals at some point? Why or why not?

3. Whether you are male or female, it's time to start noticing what you do with your legs. How do you position them when you are standing for any length of time? When you are sitting? What message do you convey with widespread legs as versus with legs pulled together? Ladies – do you sit or stand differently when you are wearing a skirt as versus trousers or shorts? Why?

4. Now it's time to notice what you do with your upper body when sitting. How do you sit in an armchair, as opposed to at a table? Try to understand your motivation for that posture. Try to analyze

what message other people are reading when they see you like that.

5. Much contradictory body language comes from being polite with people we don't like, or whom we find difficult or uncomfortable to be with. For instance, we smile only with our mouth. We don't make eye contact. We turn our torso or just our face away from the person when they are speaking to us. When you have interaction with such a person, make an honest note of your body language. Is this something you would like to change because it is sabotaging you in your job or a key relationship?

Chapter 4: Attracting Others or Distancing Yourself

Connecting with or moving away from people is not always about walking or running toward or away from someone.

You can do it with your body language –

without going anywhere with your feet. The problem is that you can only control whether you draw someone in or push him away if you master your own body language... and correctly read his!

In addition to everything you have learned in the first three chapters, we can look at some ways that work to connect with others and build rapport.

Mimicry and Imitation

If you have children in the family (or remember your own childhood), have you ever seen one of them sarcastically imitate another? In response to everything she says, he screws up his face in a sarcastic grimace and repeats it word for word, often in a singsong voice. Over and over, ad nauseam. That body language pushes her away. That body language may get him a smack on the head from his father. As you look back on this sort of scene, can you identify what the sarcastic child was really trying to communicate? Sometimes the sarcastic child is just looking for attention from the elders. Sometimes he's expressing a very low self-esteem.

Maybe most of the time, his sister just irritates him, and that's his way of expressing irritation and low-grade anger. Remember that you always need the full context to correctly read body language!

Sarcastic mimicry serves to push another person away, whatever the motivation.

But a more subtle version of imitation might just help you connect or relate to another person in quite a positive way.

Imitation, or mirroring someone's body language, when done right, communicates to the other person that you are *like him*. This message is sent nonverbally, of course. Think about it: When we are surrounded by people "like us", don't we feel more comfortable than with strangers? But beware! Don't overdo the mirroring; don't make your imitation obvious to any outside onlooker. If you're caught imitating too overtly, it will backfire on you.

Here are some examples:

You are being interviewed for a job. You have groomed and dressed quite appropriately. You have shown up on time. You have made a conscious decision to achieve positive connection with your interviewer. After all, it couldn't hurt your prospects of landing the job. When the interviewer puts her hands on the desk, after a few seconds, you place just one hand on the desk between you. If the interviewer tilts her head when she asks you a question, you pause – tilt your head ever so slightly

less than she did and respond. When she sits back her chair and lifts her chin, after a few beats, you lean back in your own chair without lifting your chin. Your mirroring has not been complete, or it has been more subtle than the interviewers. Perhaps at her next movement or gesture, you don't do anything to mirror her at all. Don't overdo it.

You are trying to impress a girl. You don't know each other very well at this point. Your decision to jump in with 2 feet on mirroring is a last minute thing. You're a bit nervous, so you end up overdoing it – immediately matching

move for move, facial expression for expression, and gesture for gesture with every single little thing she does. She has noticed this! She's not happy about it. She starts making moves away from you because you have made her so very uncomfortable. She feels like you are mocking her! Your mirroring has backfired!

Full-Body Listening

As with all body language, this may be approximate or partial in people who are listening to you – and to whom you are actively listening. To nonverbally communicate that you are listening to someone, you will essentially try to do five body language things:

1. *Sit up straight*, facing the individual, with your head in a forward facing position

2. Keep your *arms open*, rather than crossed across your chest. You might rest your forearms on a table or desk in a wide V toward the individual, or keep them propped on the arms of your armchair in a relaxed way.

3. *Lean* a bit forward all the time, or alternatively be prepared to lean forward from time to time to nonverbally show your

particular interest in a point being made. This includes interjecting with a brief "Ah, yes" or other brief comment demonstrating that you are really listening. Depending on circumstances, it might mean asking a question from time to time, which sounds something like this: "If I have understood correctly from what you have said, you mean [*blank blank blank*]. *Is that correct?*" Occasionally summarizing what the person has been saying confirms to him that you have been paying attention!

4. Make comfortable *eye contact*. Let's face it. In our North American culture, if you totally avoid eye contact, you are just

not *present* for the other individual. Those of you with your heads in your smart phones and pads all day long need to be cognizant of this. Remember, however, that this does not mean constant or piercing eye contact. Glance at the individual briefly (for a few seconds) with a relaxed face, then look away. Glance again, look away.

5. <u>Relax</u>. This might mean that you smile occasionally or even laugh. This means you are not frozen in your posture or position, but comfortably move around a little bit. Be natural. The other person will relax with you and probably express

himself more comfortably and clearly.

If you have had trouble doing this type of active listening in business or public situations, practice it at home with family and friends. You do not need to tell these individuals that you are practicing. Just do it. Try one or two of the above body positions at a time and get used to them.

Active listening, then, is not just about your ears but about your entire body's language. Active listening with supportive body language draws an individual toward you. He is attracted to you, if nothing else, as a good listener and polite individual. We could all use more of that. Doing full-body listening is appropriate in all sorts of relationships. Business people who take the time to do this are seen as leaders. Family members who do this are perceived as loving. Friends who are in the habit of doing this with you are your most trusted confidantes. Attract more people to you through full-body, active listening.

Cold Shoulder

The opposite of active, full-body listening might be the *cold shoulder*. Getting the cold shoulder from someone means they don't want to interact! They don't want to listen to you, look at you, be with you. That body language is actually quite clear: You move one shoulder physically away from the individual and keep on walking. Alternatively, you angle your body away from the person if you are seated. If someone does this to you, it is no use trying to state your verbal case now.

Do It!

1. The most private way to practice mirroring is to put a motion picture on the TV and imitate the actor's movements. Be prepared to stand and sit, stand again! (This might just be a good physical exercise program!) Perhaps you focus on different areas of the body, one after the other:

a) Mimic all the facial expressions.

b) Mimic all the arm and hand movements.

c) Imitate what the actors and actresses are doing with their legs and feet.

d) Copy them in all of the ways they lean, tilt and swivel their torsos and shoulders when standing and sitting.

e) Try to reproduce the different ways they sit down or stand up, begin a walk or draw up short after a run. You get the idea!

2. As you watch films and people in real life, model yourself on those who seem to be doing people-attracting

full-body listening. Maybe it's an interviewer who is doing more listening than interrupting.

a. Also notice their body language when an interviewer is interrupting! How is his body language, signaling that he is going to be interrupting any second now?

Chapter 5: Influencing Others

If you have read this far, you have probably conjured up pictures in your mind of the benefits of learning to read other people's body language and mastering your own.

Successful nonverbal communication, when paired with great verbal ability, undoubtedly allows you to get along with a greater number of individuals and groups than ever before. For many, "getting along better" is an end goal in and of itself. Too many of us act as though we are less than worthy of interacting with some types of

individuals – but that is an illusion!

Each of us is capable of harmonious interactions with people from all backgrounds and walks of life. Would you like to go one step further? By pursuing your mastery of your own body language and the correct reading of others' nonverbal messages, you can become a very *influential* individual!

If you are in any type of sales position or own a business, *influencing* the other person to buy is a multifaceted skill. Body language is at the core of that skillset for those of you who do face-to-face selling or presenting. But here's the catch: Only when you correctly identify the other person's body language and understand its message do you have a chance of adapting to it. Only when you master your own body language, do you have a chance of shifting into a more persuasive nonverbal way of communicating your point.

Those of you who are parents, leaders, counselors, attorneys, managers or supervisors are familiar with conflict. At home, in public and in the world of work, we see people get angry, frustrated, or stubborn. Changing the tone of your own voice to be firm but gentler than theirs can shift the energy. Refusing to mimic their angry body language, by remaining or becoming relaxed, tells them you are not impressed, not feeling at all threatened and not buying into their show. If you are comforting a young child, getting him to mimic your relaxed in-and-out breathing rhythm can help calm him down. Keeping your facial expressions neutral can be _vital_ – if you smile too much (the extreme opposite of their angry facial expression), they will think you are mocking them.

Self-confidence is very attractive and compelling to other people. It is a huge draw. As you master your personal body language more and more, you do become more confident and self-assured. They will flock to you, do virtually anything you say, believe your every word – simply because your body language expresses such confidence that you _must be saying something_ *important and valuable.* What a way to influence others to your way of thinking!

Contradiction

We have already said it: Your words match your body language or make them a lie. We communicate coherently or contradictorily. _Coherency_ means that your verbal expression (your words, and how you deliver them) and your nonverbal expression (body language) are a *match*. The nonverbal supports and reinforces the verbal and vice versa. _Contradiction_ is when they are *opposites* of each other. The verbal and nonverbal cancel each other out.

You tell your teenage kids "No smoking or drinking at that senior class party tonight at Gary's! And that's final!" But they immediately _know_ that you don't mean it. How? The parties _you_ throw at home overflow with liquor in smoke-filled rooms! Sure, you rationalize by saying you are just doing your job as a parent with that interdiction to your kids. You could be more effective by not throwing those parties while you are raising the kids. That is one option that you will probably reject out of hand! Alternatively, by wording your concern a bit differently, such as, "As we are all aware, people drink and smoke at parties. Your mom and I want you to be safe, though. We want you to stay healthy. Do you think you will be drinking? That's okay, but let's talk about that."

The boss tells a new hire that management and staff are treated on an equal footing. If this happens in a company where managers work in window offices with closed doors and the rank-and-file are in a bullpen, the boss is a liar. If this happens in a company where managers are allowed to get away with sexual harassment or creating a hostile workplace environment (but mere mortals in the staff are not), the boss is a liar – and that new employee will never take him seriously again. What would have to happen, if the boss were telling the truth? Pause for a moment and imagine the scenario.

If you seek to increase your degree of influence and credibility before others, watch for your contradictory communication and repair it! We have drawn your attention to this concept of contradiction one or two times in the Do It! sections and some of the exercises have challenged you to identify these contradictions in your personal body language. You have been identifying such incongruities in other people as well.

To be fully in integrity in your multifaceted communication with others, you may insist that contradictory body language is who and what you are. But honestly ask yourself if it is *sabotaging* your efforts to reach a goal, or to get along with key people in your life, to reach your highest potential in any number of endeavors, to feel confident in all sorts of circumstances…to influence others and be taken seriously.

Have no doubt: Influential people *learn* how to be influential with their verbal and nonverbal choices. Sure, some of them innately use the "right" body language for this. It is no secret to them, however, that *learned* body language is their secret weapon to getting people to listen to them or hear them out, to getting people to do their bidding fairly willingly.

If you were to see a film of a currently influential and successful individual from early in their career or adulthood, you might think one of two things. Either the individual was born into the right body language and has always _innately_ and subconsciously used it to his advantage. Or the person was more awkward in early years and _learned_ more useful, smooth and effective nonverbal communication as time went by. Both cases exist. You can be the one who learns and moves into smooth and effective body language that matches the words you speak. Great nonverbal mastery tells people that you are someone in integrity with yourself, someone to listen to, someone they can follow.

Influential people are taken seriously. Influential people cannot make an impact on others if their body language is contradicting their words. It's that simple. So if you are looking to influence others, you have a choice to make. You change your body language…or struggle to influence others. You change your body language to be in integrity with your words…or struggle to be taken seriously.

Consciously choosing your body language to influence someone is absolutely in your control. Like the professional actor or interviewer, you can learn to detect your unconscious body language and change it at will – it just takes practice.

Do It!

1) List the ways you and or family members' verbal and nonverbal communication contradict themselves. For each item you list, find a congruent or coherent alternative.

- For each alternative you have come up with, state how your degree of influence on other individuals has shifted (or might shift) by using this coherent rather than a contradictory approach.

2) Although this book is about body language much more than verbal communication, try to determine if some communication failure you have experienced in the past is due to your words alone, your body language alone or contradiction between the two.

   – Write down one or two benefits of developing your *verbal* communication by, for example, expanding your vocabulary or using a different tone of voice, speaking more loudly or more softly, or changing your accent.**

   – Write down two or three aspects of your body language that would – when you improve or change them – dramatically improve your ability to communicate coherently and influence others.

- Videotape yourself, or get a good friend to observe you, and note down the remaining obvious contradictions between verbal and nonverbal language.

** Margaret Thatcher is an example of a person who rose to international success and became tremendously influential – due in part by working on her voice and her body language. Her natural voice was high-pitched, even shrill, and she spoke fairly rapidly. With expert coaching, she lowered the pitch of her voice and spoke more slowly and authoritatively – and was taken more seriously. She followed advisors' guidance, wanting to be dressed in a manner that would make Britons proud. A softer, darker hairstyle and a change to a businesswoman's clothing style supported this goal achievement. She stood tall, naturally, and walked with a determined step – after all, she was in what had much been a man's world. It worked. She became a very influential leader not only in the UK but around the world during her time as Prime Minister.

Chapter 6: Success with Body Language

In many of the Do It! sections, I have encouraged you to mimic or imitate what you see in film. I have encouraged you to practice a wide range of body postures, gestures and expressions so that your repertoire of nonverbal communication via your body expands for you. In that practice, you have simply modeled yourself on someone who can do something different than you have done so far. Now it's time to model yourself on individuals that you have identified as being mesmerizing successes at nonverbal communication.

Model Yourself on Mesmerizing Success

When we listen to some public figure and say that the person "has charisma", what do we mean? That may be up for discussion, but for our purposes, it means that this individual understands how to bring together verbal and nonverbal communication to achieve *mesmerizing* results. The charismatic person takes into account emotional reactions, body signals/language, and words – combining it all to achieve his goal amongst people each and every time. It is rare for a charismatic person to be without influence! People just want to eat out of his hand and do what he asks.

The charismatic speaker or leader is not only using his body language but changing yours! He may work you up to a fever pitch of excitement. He may bring you to tears. He may convince you to take certain actions (whether you had considered them before or not). He may convince you to take a diametrically different path from the one you have been on. He uses his body language to change yours, and in the process, so very often persuades you to do things that were never before on your horizon.

People who are successful and influential tend _to avoid_ the following types of body language:

•Zero eye contact. Piercing, sustained eye contact. They just don't do it.

•Slouching when standing or sitting. Instead, they hold themselves upright to demonstrate energy and power. Similarly, they avoid weak handshakes as well as bone-crunching ones. They are not shy, and they have nothing to prove to you. They are very aware of how much pressure makes a well-received handshake.

•Creating body language barriers like arms crossed over the chest, or a crossed leg which pulls them away from your body. Quite the contrary, they are likely to create a sense of openness with their body, with loose arms and hands open and facing toward you.

•Exaggerating any of their arm or hand gestures or facial expressions. Overdoing it might communicate that they are exaggerating with their words as well – and they never feel the need to do that.

•Repeatedly looking at their smart phones, digital screens or clocks on the wall. Successful people have learned to master time and plan ahead. They tend to listen with their whole body (as discussed previously).

•Cold shouldering anybody. The successful and influential individual is fully engaged with the people he is with. He faces them, is open with them, and communicates fully with them.

•Letting involuntary tics overtake them. They either eliminate those tics or develop ways to appropriately use them.

•Invading your body space. They have more respect for you than that. This also means (as a successful and even famous personality) that they will not let you grab at them for an autograph! Reciprocity: They respect you, and you return the favor.

What this means for you is more ways to observe and correct your own body language! Mimic those who are successful and influential. The best athletes do it. The best students do it. The best leaders have done it, and continue to do it day by day.

Do It!

1. Contradictions: If you have discovered that any aspect of your body language is sabotaging you, work on it in front of a mirror.

   – First of all, eliminate that movement or facial expression through commitment and practice. Just remove it from your repertoire.

   – Secondly, decide if you need to replace it, or if removing it was sufficient to help you improve your outcomes.

2. Find a successful role model. It can be a remote relationship with no personal contact – you look

   only at the person's videos or film

   and practice. Or you can find a personal coach. Professionally trained actors or body language coaches can be found in most cities.

Conclusion

It is true that there are numerous ways to effect personal improvement. But consider that we are all continually interacting with other individuals and groups. That means we are continually communicating with others. We learned to speak before even entering

kindergarten, pretty much by mimicry –

imitating the words and speaking patterns of the people around us as we grew up. We mastered grammar and the written word, through a teacher's guidance in the classroom. But no one ever taught us about body language!

Since body language is largely cultural, first focus on learning the most effective body language of the culture you live in right now. In our multicultural USA, you may have been born and raised in a non-North American environment right here in the US

– and that is a huge asset to you! Maybe you are also carrying within you some of your family's Indonesian, Venezuelan, Ukrainian or Nigerian body language, side by side with a North American one. Having bilingual body language is just as useful in the world as being verbally bilingual! Take advantage of it. Expand upon it. Use it as a jumping board to make vast improvements in your ability to get along with individuals, influence them, attract them and understand them. Develop all your strengths and assets and go out into the world as a successful people-person!

BEFORE YOU GO

If you liked this book you may like these other books from Mark Thomas

<u>Check out more books by Mark Thomas</u>

Introduction: What you need to know about Airbnb

Airbnb Description and Features

Airbnb is an online marketplace website that allows its users to list, find and rent homes from other Airbnb users. You can list regular apartments and homes. You can also become creative with what you list. For example, one of the accommodations listed on Airbnb in NYC in 2016 was a taxi minivan parked on one of the streets of Long Island City.

You can set your availability calendar and charge what you want for your accommodation.

Obviously, you are not going to be the only Airbnb host, and you will have competition, so your pricing needs to be reasonable. However, it is a marketplace and just like in every other marketplace there are different price points and different kinds of renters and hosts.

The idea of renting space is not new. However, Airbnb and similar platforms bring a new level of convenience, speed, and transparency to it.

Why do most people rent their homes on Airbnb?

According to a study Airbnb conducted in San Francisco, the average Airbnb guest visits the city for 5.5 days and spends $1,045.

56% of the hosts said that they use Airbnb to cover mortgage or rent costs while 42% of hosts use the platform to pay for everyday living expenses.

The History Of Airbnb

As of February of 2016, Airbnb had over 60 million users. The website is active in over 192 countries, 57,000 cities and has over 500 thousand stays per night.

Airbnb was created in San Francisco in August 2008. At the time, Airbnb founders Brian

Chesky, and Joe Gebbia couldn't afford the rent for their apartment in San Francisco, and so they started renting out their living room as a bed and breakfast kind of accommodation. The room could fit three guests who used air mattresses.

In February of 2008, Airbnb's third co-founder, technical architect Nathan Blecharczyk, joined Chesky and Gebbia. In the initial stages, the founders targeted high-profile events with a shortage of lodging.

To come up with the funding for the project, the co-founders created special editions of breakfast cereals. The cereals included "Obama O's" and "Cap'n McCains," named after presidential candidates Barack Obama and John McCain. In just two months, Chesky, Blecharczyk, and Gebbia sold 800 boxes of their cereals at $40 per box, raising over $30,000.

In January of 2009, Airbnb became a part of Y Combinator's winter session that consisted of three months of training. Airbnb co-founders used the $20,000 investment they received from Y Combinator to visit New York and meet with NYC's users.

However, the company kept growing exponentially. In February of 2011, Airbnb celebrated 1 million bookings since its opening in August 2008. A little less than in a year, in January of 2012, Airbnb announced that 5 million bookings had been made through the platform. Then, in another five months, the company had 10 million nights booked. Of these bookings, 75% happened outside of the continental US.

A brief overview of requirements and things to consider when becoming an Airbnb host

To become an Airbnb host, you need to be at least 18 years old. If you plan to rent your bedroom and sleep on a couch, you need to make sure that you are willing to accept the lifestyle changes that will come with this arrangement.

Also, cleanliness is extremely important. For example, you can't have dirty laundry on the floor or your things in a mess all over the apartment. This will not be okay with your guests.

You need to be very clear and upfront about the pricing, amenities, your building, neighborhood, and expectations.

While it's not a requirement, you do want to consider investing in additional linens and towels for your guests.

On Airbnb calendar, you can block dates when your apartment is not available so that you can spend time by yourself or with your family. To keep the experience of your prospective guests positive you need to maintain an accurate calendar at all times.

When renting an entire space such as a home, apartment or a boat where you won't be on site during the stay of your guests, you need to make sure that the accommodation is prepared before a check-in, that guests can get help during check-ins and their stay at your rental and that a check-out can be performed properly.

Renting your property is a business. It may be a small scale business for you, but it's still a business.

Just like any other business, this business is not for everyone. If you are very picky about how things should be in your apartment or if you are easily annoyed by other people's habits, then this business may not be for you.

Additional details

Check with your local authorities if you are legally allowed to rent your place through Airbnb.

Airbnb is a marketplace that facilitates transactions. A transaction doesn't happen between you and Airbnb. It happens between you and your guests. It is your responsibility to make sure that such transactions are legal in your municipality.

New York City, for example, prohibits rentals of full apartments for less than 30 days. At the end of 2015, Airbnb released internal data confirming that the majority of NYC Airbnb rentals violated New York's short-term leasing laws.

In June of 2016, the New York State Senate voted to approve a bill that prohibited online advertising of short-term rentals of full apartments. The measure made it illegal to rent an entire apartment on Airbnb or any of its competitors' websites.

San Francisco legalized short-term rentals in the city on February 1, 2015. However, the law allows for rentals where a host is not present to last a maximum of 90 days a year. Violators are subject to a fine of $484 per day for first-time offenders and $968 for repeat offenders. In addition to this, hosts are required to register and apply for a permit from the Office of Short Term Rental. The fee to register is $50 for every two years. Hosts also need to apply for a business license and have liability insurance.

Check your lease to make sure that you are allowed to sublet. Even if you own your home, verify that you are not violating any homeowners' association rules.

While having furniture is not a requirement for listing a space on Airbnb, having an unfurnished accommodation will severely restrict the amount of guests that will be interested in staying at your rental.

<u>Check out more books by Mark Thomas</u>

Thank you again for downloading this book!

If you enjoyed this book, then I'd like to ask you for a favor, would you be kind enough to leave a review for this book on Amazon? It'd be greatly appreciated!

Thank you and good luck! ☺

-Mark Thomas

www.ingramcontent.com/pod-product-compliance
Lightning Source LLC
Chambersburg PA
CBHW070042210526
45170CB00012B/564